Scorpio

Also by Sally Kirkman

Aries
Taurus
Gemini
Cancer
Leo
Virgo
Libra
Sagittarius
Capricorn
Aquarius
Pisces

SALLY KIRKMAN

Scorpio

The Art of Living Well and Finding
Happiness According to Your Star Sign

HODDER

First published in Great Britain in 2018 by Hodder & Stoughton
An Hachette UK company

8

Copyright © Sally Kirkman 2018

All images © Shutterstock.com

A CIP catalogue record for this title is available from the British Library

Hardback ISBN 978 1 473 67679 4

Typeset in Celeste 11.5/17 pt by Palimpsest Book Production Limited,
Falkirk, Stirlingshire

Printed in the United States of America by LSC Communications

Hodder & Stoughton policy is to use papers that are natural,
renewable and recyclable products and made from wood grown in
sustainable forests. The logging and manufacturing processes are expected
to conform to the environmental regulations of the country of origin.

Hodder & Stoughton Ltd
Carmelite House
50 Victoria Embankment
London EC4Y 0DZ

www.hodder.co.uk

Contents

• • • • •

Introduction

·····

Before computers, books or a shared language, people were fascinated by the movement of the stars and planets. They created stories and myths around them. We know that the Babylonians were one of the first people to record the zodiac, a few hundred years BC.

In ancient times, people experienced a close connection to the earth and the celestial realm. The adage 'As above, so below', that the movement of the planets and stars mirrored life on earth and human affairs, made perfect sense. Essentially, we were all one, and ancient people sought symbolic meaning in everything around them.

We are living in a very different world now, in

which scientific truth is paramount; yet many people are still seeking meaning. In a world where you have an abundance of choice, dominated by the social media culture that allows complete visibility into other people's lives, it can be hard to feel you belong or find purpose or think that the choices you are making are the right ones.

It's this calling for something more, the sense that there's a more profound truth beyond the objective and scientific, that leads people to astrology and similar disciplines that embrace a universal truth, an intuitive knowingness. Today astrology has a lot in common with spirituality, meditation, the Law of Attraction, a desire to know the cosmic order of things.

Astrology means 'language of the stars' and people today are rediscovering the usefulness of ancient wisdom. The universe is always talking to you; there are signs if you listen and the more you tune in, the more you feel guided by life. This is one of astrology's significant benefits, helping you to make sense of an increasingly unpredictable world.

Used well, astrology can guide you in making the best possible decisions in your life. It's an essential skill in your personal toolbox that enables you to navigate the ups and downs of life consciously and efficiently.

About this book

Astrology is an ancient art that helps you find meaning in the world. The majority of people to this day know their star sign, and horoscopes are growing increasingly popular in the media and online.

The modern reader understands that star signs are a helpful reference point in life. They not only offer valuable self-insight and guidance, but are indispensable when it comes to understanding other people, and living and working together in harmony.

This new and innovative pocket guide updates the ancient tradition of astrology to make it relevant and topical for today. It distils the wisdom of the star signs into an up-to-date format that's easy to read and digest, and fun and informative too. Covering a broad range of topics, it offers you insight and understanding into many different areas of your life. There are some unique sections you won't find anywhere else.

The style of the guide is geared towards you being able to maximise your strengths, so you can live well and use your knowledge of your star sign to your advantage. The more in tune you are with your zodiac sign, the higher your potential to lead a happy and fulfilled life.

The guide starts with a quick introduction to your star sign, in bullet point format. This not only reveals your star sign's ancient ruling principles, but brings astrology up-to-date, with your star sign mission, an appropriate quote for your sign and how best to describe your star sign in a tweet.

The first chapter is called 'Be True To Your Sign' and is one of the most important sections in the guide. It's a comprehensive look at all aspects of your star sign, helping define what makes you special, and explaining how the rich symbolism of your zodiac sign can reveal more about your character. For example, being born at a specific time of year and in a particular season is significant in itself.

This chapter focuses in depth on the individual attributes of your star sign in a way that's positive and uplifting. It offers a holistic view of your sign and is meant to inspire you. Within this section, you find out the reasons why your star sign traits and characteristics are unique to you.

There's a separate chapter towards the end of the guide that takes this star sign information to a new level. It's called 'Your Cosmic Gifts and Talents' and tells you what's individual about you from your star sign perspective. Most importantly, it highlights your skills and strengths, offering you clear examples of how to make the most of your natural birthright.

The guide touches on another important aspect of your star sign, in the chapters entitled 'Your Shadow Side' and 'Your Star Sign Secrets'. This reveals the potential weaknesses inherent within your star sign, and the tricks and habits you can fall into if you're not aware of them. The star sign secrets might surprise you.

There's guidance here about what you can focus on to minimise the shadow side of your star sign, and this is linked in particular to your opposite sign of the zodiac. You learn how opposing forces complement each other when you hold both ends of the spectrum, enabling them to work together.

Essentially, the art of astrology is about how to find balance in your life, to gain a sense of universal or cosmic order, so you feel in flow rather than pulled in different directions.

Other chapters in the guide provide revealing information about your love life and sex life. There are cosmic tips on how to work to your star sign strengths so you can attract and keep a fulfilling relationship, and lead a joyful sex life. There's also a guide to your love compatibility with all twelve star signs.

Career, money and prosperity is another essential section in the guide. These chapters offer you vital information on your purpose in life, and how to make the most of your potential out in the world. Your star sign skills and strengths are revealed, including what sort of job or profession suits you.

There are also helpful suggestions about what to avoid and what's not a good choice for you. There's a list of traditional careers associated with your star sign, to give you ideas about where you can excel in life if you require guidance on your future direction.

Also, there are chapters in the book on practical matters, like your health and well-being, your food and diet. These recommend the right kind of exercise for you, and how you can increase your vitality and nurture your mind, body and soul, depending on your star sign. There are individual yoga poses and tarot cards that have been carefully selected for you.

Further chapters reveal unique star sign information about your image and style. This includes whether there's a particular fashion that suits you, and how you can accentuate your look and make the most of your body.

There are even chapters that can help you decide where to go on holiday and who with, and how to decorate your home. There are some fun sections, including ideal gifts for your star sign, and ideas for films, books and music specific to your star sign.

Also, the guide has a comprehensive birthday section so you can find out which famous people share your birthday. You can discover who else is born under your star sign, people who may be your role models and whose careers or gifts you can aspire to. There are celebrity examples throughout the guide too, revealing more about the unique characteristics of your star sign.

At the end of the guide, there's a Question and Answer section, which explains the astrological terms used in the guide. It also offers answers to some general questions that often arise around astrology.

This theme is continued in a useful section entitled Additional Information. This describes the symmetry of astrology and shows you how different patterns connect the twelve star signs. If you're a beginner to astrology, this is your next stage, learning about the elements, the modes and the houses.

View this book as your blueprint, your guide to you and your future destiny. Enjoy discovering astrological revelations about you, and use this pocket guide to learn how to live well and find happiness according to your star sign.

A QUICK GUIDE TO SCORPIO

• • • • •

Scorpio Birthdays: 24 October to 22 November

Zodiac Symbol: The Scorpion

Ruling Planet: Mars – traditional; Pluto – modern

Mode/Element: Fixed Water

Colour: Black, dark red, burgundy

Part of the Body: Genitals and reproductive system

Day of the Week: Tuesday

Top Traits: Intense, Focused, Mysterious

Your Star Sign Mission: to use your power to transformative effect in the world

Best At: magnetic attraction, wiping the slate clean, survival instincts, all-or-nothing approach to life, plumbing the depths, analysis and soul-searching, intense experiences, healing self and others

Weaknesses: obsessive, jealous, self-destructive, spiralling down, drawn towards corruption and the underworld

Key Phrase: I transform

Scorpio Quote: 'I balance the passionate, dark, insane parts of being a Scorpio the best I can.' Leonardo DiCaprio

How to describe Scorpio in a Tweet: Mysterious, complex & deep. Sex, money & death are your domain. A healer or seducer. I will survive: can start over from scratch

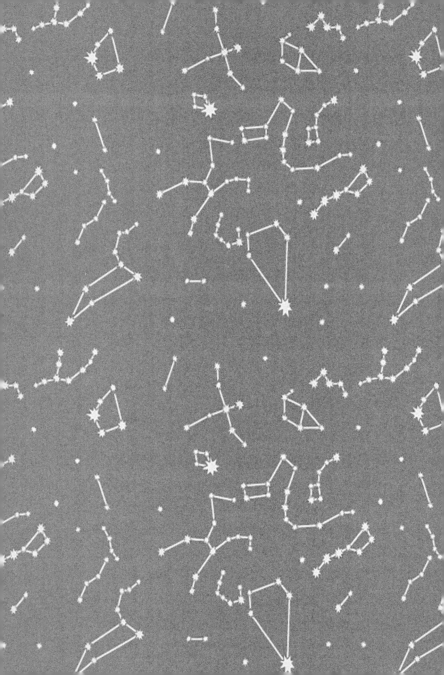

Be True To Your Sign

• • • • •

Scorpio is the sign of healing, regeneration, transformation. It rules all things taboo, among them sex, money and death. It's linked to the psyche, what's hidden, and Scorpio's keyword is power. Whether you use your power to good or bad effect in the world is down to you.

As a Scorpio you are an imposing individual, as this is the sign that rules the eighth house of the horoscope, which is the domain of death and all that is dark, hidden and mysterious. Scorpio season includes the spooky events of Halloween (31 October) and the Day of the Dead celebrations (31 October–2 November).

Halloween is a chance to dress up as ghouls or ghosts, to scare other people in a fun way. The Day of the Dead is celebrated in countries such as Mexico, when people gather at cemeteries and remember and pray for their dead loved ones, leaving them food and gifts.

Some cultures have a much closer understanding of and better relationship with death than others. Some individuals do too, and this is where your star sign excels.

Many Scorpios instinctively understand that good and evil coexist in the world and that the dark side of life is as necessary as the light. The day wouldn't exist without the night and, in the natural world, all that grows also decays.

Scorpio is the sign of regeneration, connected inextricably to the cycles of nature; growth, full bloom and dying and the human cycle of birth, life and death. In the northern hemisphere, the Sun's move into Scorpio takes us deeper into winter, the time of the year after the harvest, when plants and nature are starting to die back and close down.

The dead leaves and plant waste turn into mulch in the ground, nature's way of recycling and creating compost. This is nature's method of giving discarded matter back to the earth in preparation for life to be reborn in the spring.

In a similar pattern, detox, purging and decluttering are essential Scorpio strategies, paring life back to basics so you can wipe the slate clean ready to start over. Your ultimate Scorpio goal is transformation in all its guises.

As a key eighth house theme, death is often a significant issue in a Scorpio's life. This can range from a fascination with death, bereavement experiences in formative years right through to mediumship, psychic abilities or an affinity with the paranormal.

In some way, shape or form, you as a Scorpio will embrace or come into contact with the dark side of life, even if you just wear black clothes or you read poems and novels about death or loss. A typical Scorpio knows that periods of introversion, crisis and even despair can play a vital role in your personal growth and self-development.

A potent symbol associated with your sign is the phoenix, the mythical firebird, which dies and is reborn from the ashes. Many Scorpios start from scratch at some point in their lives, and it's your ability to change your own and other people's lives for the better that defines the real essence of your sign.

Being a Scorpio, you have two ruling planets. Your traditional ruler is the masculine planet Mars, god of war, which symbolises the cut and thrust of life. The red planet suggests heat and is linked to anger, passion and pain. Mars lends you your determined nature, your steely focus in life and your ambition.

The other planet associated with Scorpio is Pluto, named after the god of the underworld. Pluto was discovered in 1930, and world events and developments at the time of a planet's discovery can reveal a lot about the planet's symbolism. This was a crucial period in two particular fields: nuclear power and the birth of psychoanalysis.

Nuclear energy generates power but is not without its dangers, inherent both in the radioactive waste it produces and in the greater fear of annihilation. Power is a Scorpio concept, but it's how you wield your power that is all-important.

This is a crucial point to note for you as a Scorpio because you are the one who can decide how to use your power. You can choose to channel it into activities that benefit yourself, and the greater good, or you can use your power in a way that can be self-destructive or dangerous to other people or even to life itself. So there is an extreme nature to your Scorpio character.

The world of psychoanalysis also belongs to Scorpio. Your unconscious symbolises your own underworld, a place of shadows and buried experiences that can be unearthed and healed through the psychoanalytic process.

Many Scorpios are fascinated with the unconscious and what makes people tick and you often pride yourself on your ability to read other people. Your sign goes beyond the obvious, and you make natural therapists, healers and sleuths.

Classic Scorpio archetypes are the detective and the researcher who's willing to go to any lengths to reveal what's hidden. You're not scared of venturing into taboo territory either, and sex, money, power and the afterlife are all associated with your sign.

Secrets are an integral part of your character, and if you're typical of Scorpio, you will be notoriously private. You don't like to give a lot away, and even if you walk the path of fame, you're likely to shun the limelight and keep your private life separate from your public life.

Scorpio is a fixed water sign and water represents the emotions in astrology. The fixed mode holds firm, stable and steadfast, meaning that you can plumb the depths of your own feelings, but you're not always readily emotional around others. Those volcanic depths bubble away until they erupt with force.

As a Scorpio, you are more than capable of transcending darkness to emerge into the light stronger and wiser for your experience. A typical Scorpio will take on any challenge with a rare combination of determination and laser focus.

When you throw yourself into a project, a relationship, a lifelong goal, you do so with wholehearted passion. It is this ability to fixate on a goal or cause that can make you so successful in your endeavours.

Your Shadow Side

Scorpios are often branded with the worst reputation of the zodiac. Ask anyone what they know about your sign, and they're likely to reply with some or all of the following epithets: sex-mad, dangerous, power-crazy, evil!

Admittedly, Scorpio is the sign of the zodiac that's associated with life's taboos including sex, money, power and death. There can be strength, though, in your fascination for the dark side of life, and you are courageous enough to venture into the unknown and unfamiliar territory.

This is where you have to be careful, because there is a flip side and some Scorpios wander too far into dangerous or taboo territory. Remember that how you use your power is all-important, and steer yourself away from the abuse of power or falling into corruption. A world of crime or evil can be a spiralling descent into the underworld with no escape.

All signs learn from their opposite in the zodiac and for you, this is Taurus, one of the earth signs. A typical Taurus has both feet firmly planted on the ground and lives in the real world. If you ever find yourself spiralling into Scorpio darkness, whether on an inner or outer level, bring yourself back to everyday matters and real life. Return to basics and sound values.

There will be times when your extreme Scorpio nature wants to dive into the dark but it's imperative to keep sight of the light. Don't forget either that part of Scorpio's greatness lies in your ability to be reborn, to reinvent yourself.

It's worth noting that there are two other symbols belonging to Scorpio. The first is the eagle, which represents your ability to soar high, to be magnificent in life. The eagle is a symbol of strength and power.

The second is the serpent, immortalised in the tale of Adam and Eve. The serpent deceives Eve into eating fruit from the forbidden tree, which she then shares with Adam. This rewards them with knowledge but also the harmful and destructive concepts of shame and evil. So the serpent symbolises sin.

That is only one half of the story because the serpent is also a symbol of fertility, the creative life force, rebirth and transformation (it sheds its skin) and healing. These are Scorpio's strengths, and the symbol of the serpent, in particular, reveals the extremes inherent in your character. Choose wisely, especially if you dare to walk on the dark side.

Your Star Sign Secrets

Shhh, don't tell anyone but your greatest fear is losing control. You gain inner strength from the knowledge that ultimately you hold power in your life and can take charge not only of yourself but of other people as well. You find it hard to let other people make critical decisions for you, or even to ask for help. This is Scorpio's star sign secret.

There's another secret too, which is that you don't like to reveal a lot about yourself, certainly not

when you first meet someone. Knowledge =
power to the Scorpio mind and you can be very
good at getting the truth out of other people, but
you rarely give a lot away.

Your Love Life

> **KEY CONCEPTS:** seductive power, soulmate attraction, intense relationships, jealousy and revenge, undying love

Cosmic tip: a Scorpio relationship that doesn't include a healthy sex life rarely lasts.

Knowing about your star sign is an absolute essential when it comes to love and relationships. Once you understand what drives you, nurtures you and keeps you happy in love, then you can be true to who you are rather than try to be someone you're not.

Plus, once you recognise your weak points when it comes to relationships (and everyone has them), you can learn to moderate them and focus instead on boosting your strengths to find happiness in love.

It's sometimes said that power is the ultimate aphrodisiac, and Scorpios have a legendary sex drive. If you're a typical Scorpio, a dashing mix of passion, dedication and determination combined with charisma and an awareness of your sexual power can be completely intoxicating.

The classic female Scorpio archetype is the femme fatale, which translated means 'deadly woman', but has come to stand more broadly for an alluring and seductive female.

Scorpio is one of the feminine signs and, coupled with your renowned magnetism, it's no surprise that you have a reputation for being vampish and enticing, the men as well as the women.

The original femme fatale was Scorpio Vivien Leigh (5 November), who shot to fame playing Scarlett O'Hara in one of the most iconic films of all time, *Gone With The Wind* (1939). She wasn't the favourite to win the lead role, but after her screen test she was praised for her extreme wildness.

There isn't a male equivalent of the epithet 'femme fatale', but that's not to say that Scorpio men are any less seductive. The legendary actor Richard Burton (10 November) is the classic example of a libidinous male Scorpio.

This was partly due to his on-off relationship with the Pisces actress Elizabeth Taylor, one of the most famous love stories. They shared a cosmic marriage in astrology because Taylor's Moon in Scorpio was at the same point in the zodiac as Burton's Sun in Scorpio.

There are no half measures when you're born under the sign of Scorpio and intensity is one of your hallmarks. When you're interested in someone, they know immediately by the way you look at them. Your piercing eyes sizzle with intensity, and it may feel to the other person, the object of your affection, that they've been hypnotised or entranced. You're a genius at magnetic attraction.

Consequently, you have something of a reputation for being a sexual predator, but when it comes to love, you are on a quest to find your soulmate. Any love relationship that's going to last has to go deep.

Admittedly, your traditional planet Mars rules the libido, but contrary to expectation or popular belief, the majority of Scorpios tend not to seek out a one-night stand. As you are one of the emotional water signs, sex without love, intimacy or a deep connection doesn't hold your fascination for long.

This is because you're inquisitive about the human psyche. Both enigmatic and secretive, you have an inner knowingness, a natural intuition, and you are constantly looking for clues and evidence to another person's character and motivations. In a love relationship, you want to know everything about your other half.

So forget superficial relationships or half-hearted affairs. It's all or nothing in love, as in life, for your passionate sign. You don't tend to fall in love quickly, but when you do, you commit wholeheartedly and expect the same in return. In fact, you are one of the most loyal signs of the zodiac and mutual trust is an essential ingredient in love if a relationship is to last.

Relationships are an intense experience for your sign of Scorpio as you feel both love and hurt deeply. When you love deeply, this includes tension as Mars, your ruling planet, governs anger in addition to lust and sexuality.

It is your ability to give yourself over totally to love, and to expect the same in return, that arouses strong emotions. This is especially evident for you when a relationship is in trouble or comes to an untimely end.

Being a fixed sign, you are unusually tenacious and can find it hard to let go. Add to this the fact that you are fearless about your own 'dark side' and you get a better sense of why you suffer when love hurts.

Many Scorpios go through a phase in their lives when love and obsession go hand in hand. This can range from torturing yourself about your partner's ex-relationships to stalking someone who refuses to show an interest in you or loving the one you're with wholeheartedly to the exclusion of everything else in your life, for a while at least.

How you deal with a relationship break-up does mark you out as unique. If someone slights you or mistreats you, your own reactions can be extreme. It's quite common for you as a Scorpio to cut yourself off from another person entirely if you experience too much pain or rejection. There can be no going back.

The other side of your nature has a lot to do with your zodiac symbol, the scorpion, and its legendary sting in the tail. Many of you will have your own tale of revenge or guilty jealous secrets.

In fact, the phrase 'hell hath no fury like a woman scorned' could have been written for you and applies to both sexes. This is where your wicked Scorpio side can kick in as you plot your revenge.

Once you know what extremes you are capable of going to, all in the name of love, ensure that you venture boldly and daringly into the love arena. This remains one area in your life where you can experience a soulmate connection and that, for you, is one of the best experiences.

The traditional marriage vow contains the line 'till death us do part' and that means a lot to your Scorpio nature. You desire a love connection that's going to last, which is perhaps one of the reasons why you don't commit casually.

If you want to get a feel for what Scorpio love is all about, watch the cult movie *The Notebook* (2004). It's about star-crossed lovers, fate that intervenes, feeling pain as well as pleasure, knowing that love and destiny are connected as one.

The movie incorporates classic Scorpio themes and the two actors who play the leading roles, Ryan Gosling (12 November) and Rachel McAdams (17 November), are both Sun Scorpio.

Your Love Matches

Some star signs are a better love match for you than others. The classic combinations are the other two star signs from the same element as your sign, water; in Scorpio's case, Cancer and Pisces.

If a relationship is too relaxed, however, you might find you lose interest quickly. You need a partner by your side who's willing to explore the depths of life and who will go to any lengths to ensure you're a match made in heaven.

It's also important to recognise that any star sign match can be a good match if you're willing to learn from each other and use astrological insight to find out more about what makes the other person tick. Here's a quick guide to your love matches with all twelve star signs.

Scorpio–Aries: Soulmates

Both your star signs are ruled by the planet Mars, god of war. This is an intense, passionate combination that often leads to a competitive relationship; two active individuals who are as determined and steely as each other.

Scorpio–Taurus: Opposites Attract

Scorpio is associated with life's hidden riches, intrigued by the metaphysical realm, whereas Taurus rules money and the physical world. Scorpio brings depth and intensity to the relationship and Taurus grounds Scorpio in the real world.

Scorpio–Gemini: Soulmates

Scorpio and Gemini is an intriguing combination as you both love to seek knowledge and find things out. Life is a mystery to be explored to the full, but sometimes you need a break from each other as your sign is deep and intense whereas Gemini is chatty and light.

Scorpio–Cancer: In Your Element

You two can be content cut off from the rest of the world. You share a capacity for intimacy, plus you both enjoy quiet times and having a place you can retreat to away from the outside world. If you keep the waves of emotion flowing freely, you can happily set up home together.

Scorpio–Leo: Squaring Up To Each Other

This is a match based on power as both of you are keen to make your mark on the world. Leo seeks out the light whereas Scorpio searches in dark places. If you allow each other to rule in your own ways, this can be a proud and powerful pairing.

Scorpio–Virgo: Sexy Sextiles

Scorpio's laser focus meets Virgo's perfectionist high standards, and you two can get lost picking out the details rather than focusing on the bigger picture. Both signs have hidden depths, however, and once unleashed this match can be a hotbed of pulsating passion.

Scorpio–Libra: Next-Door Neighbours

Ruled by Mars and Venus respectively, Scorpio and Libra are cosmic lovers. A tempestuous but loving match, this love affair can reach mythic proportions. Issues may arise if you want to go in deep as Libra prefers to keep love light.

Scorpio–Scorpio: Two Peas In A Pod

Two Scorpios are a passionate and erotic combination. This pairing is intense as Scorpio goes in deep and needs a soulmate connection. Once a Scorpio gives their heart, love is loyal and genuine. Together for ever; till death us do part.

Scorpio–Sagittarius: Next-Door Neighbours

You both thrive on adventure, so there's no shortage of passion between you. In the long term, you want love to be intense and seek a psychic connection, whereas freedom-loving Sagittarius wants love to be fun, and commitment can be an issue.

Scorpio–Capricorn: Sexy Sextiles

You both feel fulfilled ticking off life goals or significant achievements. Love tends to be a slow burn as neither of you favours a quick fling over a deep and meaningful connection. If you share a similar philosophy on life, your love can grow and mature like a fine red wine.

Scorpio–Aquarius: Squaring Up To Each Other

Together the two of you can go on a magical mystery tour and discover places that other people don't even know exist. At your best, you two connect on a deep level and are interested in pushing back the boundaries of knowledge.

Scorpio–Pisces: In Your Element

When you combine passion and intensity (Scorpio) with romance and bliss (Pisces), you have a relationship of epic proportions. A massive wave of love washes back and forth between you. You both understand that sometimes it's through pleasure and pain that you experience life most fully.

Your Sex Life

• • • • •

Erotic rather than sensual, oozing with sexuality rather than overtly sexy; being a Scorpio, you have your own unique blend of sexual magnetism and exploring your sexuality to the full is an integral part of your life's journey.

For you, sex is something far more important than merely the physical act. Sex has almost mystical or sacred meaning in your eyes, and you make love in such a way as to raise a purely physical act to spiritual heights.

It's easy for a lover to become obsessed or entranced by you because you move in such a secretive manner. You hold your cards close to your chest and enjoy the thrill of knowing glances, illicit sex and carefully timed touch with words unspoken.

Your sexual repertoire can never be termed ordinary. It may hold a trace of cruelty, a hint of masochism and fantasies that your mother never knew existed. Out of all the star signs, you're the one most likely to enjoy bondage and dressing up in full kinky gear. The S&M world unites pain and pleasure, and it's another version of the Scorpio underworld.

You understand the link between sex and power, and even if your lover is powerful in their own right out in the world, at times they must be willing to be submissive to your demands in private. You leave your mark, for no one can come into contact with you so intimately and not come out of it without having experienced life in much more depth.

Scorpio rules the genitals, and you love dramatic, unusual sex positions where your lover has full and easy access to every part of you and vice versa.

Many Scorpios go through a period in their life-time when their libido drops, usually at an older age. This again indicates the extreme nature of Scorpio, when even sex can be an all-or-nothing affair. Sometimes it's when you're denied some-thing in life that your desire for it builds once again. Once passion reignites in your world, it tends to do so in explosive fashion and age is no boundary.

A common term for an orgasm in French is 'la petite mort', which translated literally means 'little death', and there's an obvious reference here that links to your sign. When it is seen as an act of complete surrender, the sexual is elevated to some-thing special. You give yourself up 100% to the experience.

Consider sex in this way, and it becomes a portal through which you consciously lose control at the point of orgasm. You let go completely and at some level you 'die' for that moment, only to re-emerge and be reborn. Sharing this experience with someone you love elevates the act of love-making to that of a regenerative or healing union.

SCORPIO ON A FIRST DATE

- You enter the dating arena in full seductive mode

- You listen more to the other person than you reveal about yourself

- You want to know about their wild side

- You like to portray an air of mystery

- Your intensity can scare some people away

Your Friends and Family

Friendships are important to you, but you don't necessarily make friends quickly. You need people in your life who you can connect with on a deep level, and idle gossip or chatter rarely does it for you. So in friendships as in life, you'll go on a quest to seek out the very best, the people who add something to your life rather than leave you feeling depleted.

You don't want to expend too much energy on

finding friends either; instead, you trust in fate that the right people will come along at the right time. A lot of your close connections do have a sense of destiny about them, e.g. meeting someone coincidentally a second time if you didn't hook up first time round.

Once you've found your close friends in life, then, like all Scorpio relationships, you expect to be friends for ever and a day. Even if you don't see one another a lot, a good friend will slot back into your life as if you'd never been apart. Once you know someone on a soul level, that never leaves you.

You're not usually the type of person who needs a friend in your life twenty-four seven. You like your own space, and you quickly feel drained of energy if someone wants to be around all the time. Instead, you tend to have different friends who feed different parts of your personality, and each one is as important as the next.

Big social gatherings and small talk are rarely your thing. In fact, for some Scorpios, this can be your worst nightmare. You hate anything too frivolous or trivial, and that includes small talk and light conversation.

Instead, you'd rather have a few great friends who you see on a one-to-one basis. This allows for intimate conversation and a deep connection, getting to know one another in a way that you couldn't if you always socialised in a group context.

You do have certain rules and guidelines that cannot be crossed when it comes to friendship and revealing your secrets is one of them. It can be a death knell to a friendship if you tell something in confidence and then find out that a so-called friend has been gossiping behind your back. For a typical Scorpio, a promise is a promise and should never be broken. You would never reveal a friend's secret or confidence.

From your own point of view, you do have to be careful that you don't become overly possessive with your close friends. You can find it hard to deal with if your best friend partners up and you don't get on with their other half. You won't be impressed either if you get edged out and your friendship is relegated to a lower priority.

You could even end up issuing an ultimatum to a friend if you feel strongly enough: it's your partner or me, make your choice. Once a friendship is broken, it's rare that a Scorpio will go back or try again.

When it comes to family, you often have an independent relationship with them. If you're a typical Scorpio, you won't be tied to your mother's apron strings, but instead, you'll be ready to leave home and start your own life.

This doesn't mean that you can't have a close relationship with your parents or siblings, but you do need to stand on your own two feet and find your own place in life. Whether you remain close or not depends on how much you have in common with your family. Any relationship has to bring with it a certain amount of interest, fascination or learning to keep you engaged.

One factor that does create close ties with your family members is humour and especially dark humour. This is where you can be truly weird and express the full range of your personality, and your family often love you for it.

Facing adversity together with family also creates a close bond. In fact, any intense experience that you go through with a loved one or people close to you can transform your relationship, often for the better.

Not every Scorpio will want to have their own family. Sometimes you value your own independence, or you have a different purpose in life that you want to fulfil. If you do become a parent, more likely than not you will fight tooth and nail to protect and look after your children.

You might not want a huge brood but, instead, choose to have a close relationship with one child born to you or a child who comes into your life some other way. This is where your Scorpio power can be formidable. As a parent, you want the very best for your kids, and you will move heaven and earth to ensure they are happy and live well.

Your Health and Well-Being

KEY CONCEPTS: holistic well-being –
mind, body and soul, exercise as release,
mind control, cleansing and elimination

What's important to remember with your sign of
Scorpio is that you are an extreme character, and
one thing you often have to learn to stay fit and
healthy is to adopt the mantra 'All things in moder-
ation.' Your natural approach to food is to be a

faster or a feaster rather than someone who eats sensibly on a daily basis.

In addition, you're one of the emotional water signs, so how you feel emotionally will matter a lot to whether you're living well. You can quickly go off the rails if you spiral into self-destructive mode, whether your vice is alcohol, drugs, sex or rich food.

It is important therefore to channel your intense emotions and your fierce spirit into activities that make you feel good. You might aim high for a black belt in karate or beat a squash ball aggressively around the court to release tension. You might be drawn more towards eastern disciplines, such as t'ai chi or Thai boxing. Water sports are likely to appeal to your water sign nature too.

You like to be in tip-top physical condition, whatever your age, as you can't be a formidable Scorpio if you're weak in your body. Plus, you have the determination and perseverance to commit yourself body and soul to a fitness programme or a walking or running challenge. You attack any personal goal head-on with your usual high levels of willpower and strength.

Sometimes it's a crisis in your own life that acts as a wake-up call and necessitates you completely transforming your way of living. If you're typical of your sign, you tend to push yourself to the limit in the pursuit of your chosen goals. This can lead to a breakdown if you take it too far, so rein in your compulsive nature before it impacts on your well-being.

Control of the mind is often a Scorpio fascination, and your mind and subconscious is an area that is worth exploring to the full. Whatever your personal belief in the power of the mind to transform your life, it's here where you can often achieve mastery.

It might lead you down the road of NLP, meditation or other disciplines that allow you to steer your mind in the way you choose. This is especially important if you're the type of Scorpio who can spiral down into negative thinking. Every now and again you need to take time out, so head for a retreat or go off on your own to a place of quiet and solitude.

One of the best ways of enjoying yourself and letting go is to dance and release your inhibitions. Your sexual energy is intense, and dances such as salsa or tango are a Scorpio's dream. The more in touch you are with your sexual power, the easier it is for you to tap into your creative and spiritual sources.

Your sign of Scorpio rules the genitals and the reproductive system; in fact, any part of the body that's involved in procreation and excretion. It is important for you to look after your sexual health and to ensure you practise safe sex.

You don't always trust in conventional medicine, or at least you will often consider alternative therapies in addition to traditional methods. You're likely to take a holistic view of your health.

As a classic Scorpio, you may also have a strong response to periods in your life when your hormones are changing. This includes puberty and the menopause. At these times, it's a good idea to take extra vitamins or minerals that will help stabilise you and rebalance any extreme symptoms.

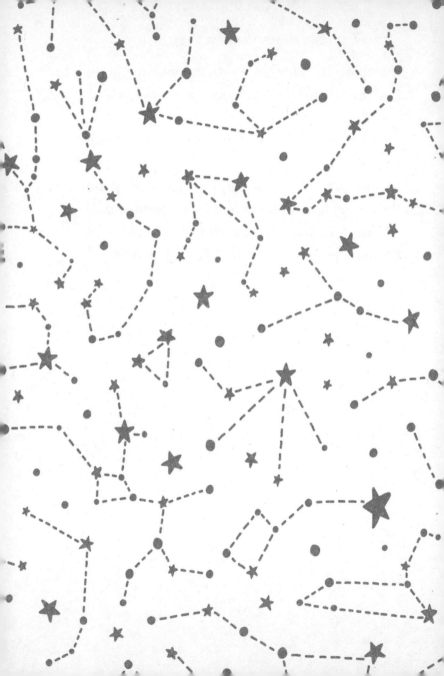

Scorpio and Food

When it comes to food, you tend to know what you like and what's good for you, even if this means you veer towards a special diet. As a Scorpio, you often know your body well.

If you have any specific digestive ailments or, for Scorpio women, menstrual problems, you will delve deep to discover what you need to eat or not eat to keep yourself healthy.

You're not afraid to try foods that are out of the ordinary, whether you have a taste for offal, only eat organic food or are a vegan. Whatever diet you choose, it will be because it works for you and is unique to you. You're not a faddy eater as such, but you do know your own mind.

You can be a compulsive eater at times, and you may go through stages in your life when you love nothing more than drinking to excess. As with all things in life, you're willing to push the boundaries, and it's often the sensation of being drunk, even out of control, that you want to explore. Red wine tends to be a Scorpio favourite, and sometimes strong spirits. You might go through a phase of smoking to release nervous tension.

Atmosphere is important to you when it comes to eating, and a dark restaurant hideaway lit by candlelight suits your emotional Scorpio nature. Ideally, you'll be with a single companion, but a typical Scorpio won't mind eating out on their own.

Food is a sensual experience for you, and you're likely to know off by heart which foods are aphrodisiacs, e.g. oysters and dark chocolate.

Mars is the planet that rules Scorpio food, including spicy herbs and vegetables, such as onions, chillies, garlic, basil and peppers. Fermented foods are ideal for Scorpio too, such as pickles, well-hung game and blue cheeses. Also prunes or a high-fibre diet that helps to keep you regular and aid your digestion.

Cleansing and elimination are good for Scorpio, to release toxins, whether you choose to detox, have a colonic irrigation or fast. You're unlikely to veer towards a stringent diet, however, because your attitude towards both food and drink is that it should be indulged and enjoyed. Little and often is a better approach for you than never at all.

Do You Look Like A Scorpio?

Scorpios are renowned for their intense stare and magnetic attraction. Your eyes have a laser focus, and other people can experience the way you look at them as if you're gazing directly into their soul.

In response, you tend to give nothing or little away, and your own persona can be described as enigmatic and mysterious. Your profile is primarily dark and brooding, exuding passion and intensity.

Female Scorpios often have an ice maiden beauty that suggests you can look, but you can't touch.

Dark or jet black hair is the classic Scorpio style although you do find platinum blonde Scorpios. You like your look to be extreme and will often experiment with different hair colours and styles.

The archetypal Scorpio has strong facial features and prominent cheekbones. You walk with confidence and rarely slouch. When you enter a room, you can be silent and other people will still sense your presence and turn towards you.

Your Style and Image

Most Scorpios look good in black, and it's not unusual for you to go through a 'black' phase at least once in your lifetime. This might be during your teenage years when you like to dress as a goth, or perhaps you're the type of female Scorpio who knows that no outfit works as well as the LBD, the little black dress.

Add some killer heels and a slash of dark red lipstick and you have an outfit that suggests sex and power, two of your favourite things. Scorpio men can achieve a similar effect in a classic dark suit or black jeans and a polo neck jumper. Think of the 'James Bond' school of styling and you won't go far wrong.

Accessories are there to act as a statement; fussy and frivolous are out, eye-catching and dramatic are in. Silver tends to be your choice of jewellery rather than gold, but you only need one stunning belt or necklace in a unique style for you to stand out.

It's also the items that other people can't see and what's hidden to the naked eye that often say a lot about your sign of Scorpio. Sexy black lingerie, suspenders or a discreet tattoo that will only be revealed when your clothes are unzipped.

Simple, classic lines suit you well, and luxurious fabrics not only look great but also feel good on your skin: velvet and satin, for example. You often prefer a few quality pieces in your wardrobe rather than too much clutter or confusion. And a fitted leather jacket, preferably in black or burgundy, is the quintessential Scorpio statement piece.

Dark glasses are a must, and you can never have too many pairs, not only to wear outside in the sun but to wear inside as well, to give off a sense of allure.

The Scorpio icon for the dark glasses look is Anna Wintour (3 November), editor of American *Vogue* magazine and one of the power women of New York, who is rarely missing from the front row of the top fashion shows. Her look is classic Scorpio with her trademark bob and classic suits.

One thing to remember when it comes to Scorpio style is that you are a genius at transformation. A star with her own eclectic style is the singer-songwriter Björk (21 November), who has both the Sun and Moon in Scorpio. Björk changes her look as frequently as she changes her musical style.

Even just a new haircut and colour or an outfit different from your usual style not only keeps other people guessing but allows you to take on a new personality whenever you choose. Not being recognised gives you the privacy that you crave. Dark glasses on – check; coat collar turned up high – check: you're ready for the outside world.

Your Home

Your Ideal Scorpio Home:

Privacy and intimacy are key concepts for your dream home, and you need somewhere quiet you can hide away. An ideal choice would be the private island of Skorpios in Greece, currently owned by the Onassis family.

Walking into a Scorpio's home can create a sense of unfamiliarity. If anyone's going to live exactly as they want and defy convention, it's your sign. Your definition of style is uniquely your own, and you rarely care a fig for what other people think. In fact, you're happiest when you provoke a strong reaction from others, rather than indifference.

Your home is unlikely to be light or particularly airy. You love the dark and much prefer hidden and intimate surroundings to too much space.

If you're a true Scorpio, you have an eye for the unusual, and you love to collect weird and wonderful objects. A clean, white and bright environment is not classic Scorpio. The colours associated with your sign are black and dark red, dramatic colours that make a statement.

Pluto, your co-ruler, was god of the underworld in mythology, another reason why you like your home to be a place of privacy. Often you need your own space and enjoy times of solitude. Your home must have a den, corner or alcove where you can be alone. Secret nooks and crannies where you can hide away are ideal for you.

Leather and dark wood suit your Scorpio style and old pieces of furniture that have a history appeal to your sense of mystery. Fabrics will ideally be dark velvets and thick drapes. Most Scorpios love anything gothic, and old candelabra and high-backed chairs often have pride of place in your living room.

You have a fascination with the dark side of life, and this often shows in some of the weirder items you pick up in junk shops or on your travels to far-flung places in the world.

You're often interested in the paranormal and a typical Scorpio isn't scared of superstition or anything forbidden. This is often revealed in what's lying around your home, whether you collect primitive masks or you have a stone torso in the living room. You often own a stand-out object that is a real talking point because it's so unusual.

Scorpio is a sensual sign, and you like your home surroundings to be evocative, a place where people can revel in the senses. You love strong scents like musk or sandalwood and candles are the ideal way to light a Scorpio room. There are often certain items in your possession too that have a strong emotional connection for you, such as CDs or books.

Your bedroom is often an intimate haven, although your tastes may be too dramatic for some, especially if you opt for dark red and black as your colour scheme. With smart use of lighting, evocative scents and luxurious fabrics, it will certainly be a place for passion.

Your favourite room is often the bathroom, with a big bath you can languish in with a glass of red wine as you read a thriller or detective novel by candlelight. You can also be just as content lounging in front of a real fire with a few trusted friends or enjoying intimate moments with your loved one in the bedroom.

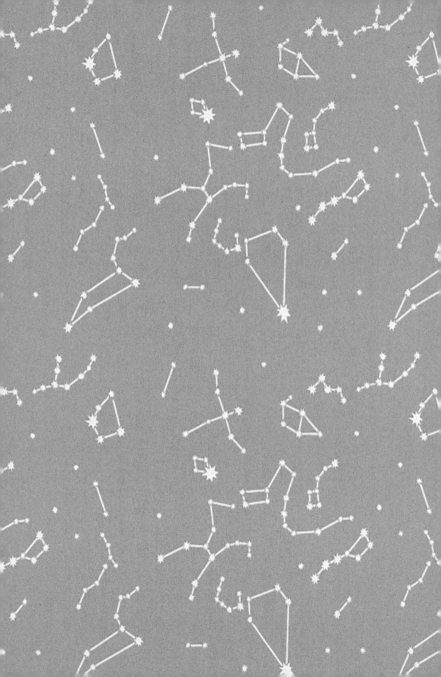

Your Star Sign Destinations

IDEAS FOR SCORPIO:

- *a stay in a riad in Morocco*

- *explore the ancient mysteries of Glastonbury*

- *visit New Orleans for the jazz and voodoo*

Did you know that many cities and countries are ruled by a particular star sign? This is based on when a country was founded, although, depending on their history, sometimes places have more than one star sign attributed to them.

This can help you decide where to go on holiday, and it can also be why there are certain places where you feel at home straight away.

Anywhere exotic and mysterious will appeal to your Scorpio nature and you often enjoy exploring cultures that are completely alien to your own. You're happy to blend in too, to wear traditional clothes, try out the local cuisine and immerse yourself completely in the new experience.

You love to venture into unexplored territory or find your very own secret hideaway that no one else knows about. The last thing you want to do is to broadcast your top holiday finds to other people. A beach that's packed to the hilt is usually your idea of holiday hell.

Water has a soothing influence on you and being by the sea calms your soul, ideally in a place where you can be happy relaxing and watching the light as it changes throughout the day. If you're typical of your sign of Scorpio, you will love watching the sunset too, as day turns to night, or lying under the night stars gazing at the constellations.

Somewhere you can disappear on your own often suits your elusive, hidden nature. Hot springs and places with healing powers attract you. Having sex in an exotic location has also got to be high up the Scorpio wish list, whether you're with your lover or an exotic stranger.

Countries ruled by Scorpio include Morocco, Brazil, Norway, Algeria, Korea, the Transvaal and German Bavaria

Cities ruled by Scorpio include Liverpool, Halifax and Hull in the UK; New Orleans and Washington DC in the USA; Rio de Janeiro in Brazil; Fez in Morocco; Ghent in Belgium; Catalonia and Valencia in Spain

Your Career and Vocation

KEY CONCEPTS: taboo careers   sex,
death and money – the power magnate,
laser focus, fulfilling your purpose,
healing and transformation

As a Scorpio, it's important to find a career that
you can immerse yourself in 100%, and there's
no reason why you shouldn't aim high in life.
After all, your two ruling planets, Mars and Pluto,

are connected to ambition and power and, at your best, you can make your mark on the world.

Some Scorpios achieve positions of high status, which comes with the responsibility of power. Power is your domain, and it can suit your sign's nature to be in a situation where you have ultimate control. Transformation is an essential Scorpio concept, and some Scorpios become key figures in politics or environmental affairs, where they can influence the development and growth of society and the world.

Scorpio governs big business and wealth. With your capacity for ferocious ambition coupled with an ability to stay fixed on your goals to the point of obsession, it's no surprise to find some big Scorpio hitters in this area, with the founder of Microsoft, Bill Gates (28 October) at the top of the list. He was number one on Forbes' list of 'The World's Richest People' for fifteen consecutive years.

It's power rather than the acquisition of money that tends to drive the ambitious side of your Scorpio nature. Scorpio women often thrive in male-oriented industries. A good example in the States are the two powerful women Hillary Clinton (26 October) and Condoleezza Rice (14 November), who've either taken on or gone for major roles in US government.

There are other areas where Scorpio men and women both fare well, and the finance industry is one of them. This isn't necessarily about personal money either but about trading money, stocks and shares and hedge funds. If you're a typical Scorpio, you will have nerves of steel, and you're often cool under pressure. This means you can make intelligent decisions even when it comes to dealing with millions of pounds.

The sex industry is another area where Scorpios often excel, and this doesn't mean selling sex – unless you have a real-life fantasy to be a dominatrix. Instead you are more likely to take on a leading role in the sex industry, where you have control and power over what happens.

A typical Scorpio recognises that sex is natural and vital to human existence, even if the sex industry contains many taboos. Scorpios often push the boundaries where sex is concerned and are willing to test people's limits and challenge their expectations. There are some key Scorpio individuals, both male and female, who've played a key role in the lucrative pornography and sex publications industries.

The other 'taboo' area associated with your sign is death, which can lead to some exciting career options. If you're a typical Scorpio, you won't be squeamish but will be able to handle blood or even working with dead bodies; as a forensic pathologist or undertaker, for example, or someone who works with people who are dying, such as in a hospice or as a bereavement counsellor.

You more than any other sign are often willing to

hold and process painful emotions. You can delve into the dark places that frighten other people, which is why all forms of therapy fascinate you. Finding out what makes people tick is something you do well, so doing it as a career is a natural progression.

You're also renowned as the detective of the zodiac and any career that involves research or sleuthing suits your Scorpio nature. Your concentration levels tend to be high, especially if whatever you're dealing with holds your interest.

If you have a tight deadline to meet, you can home in with your laser focus to get things done in time. Your ruler Mars represents speed, while Pluto enables to you to go in deep and penetrate to the heart of the matter.

Attention to detail is another Scorpio skill, and you are strong in a career that requires precision work. Sometimes you have to learn when to stop, however, as your perfectionist streak can turn into an obsession.

Ideally, you want your working environment to be a place that's quiet or at least have your own office or a corner where you can hide away. You only tend to have so much patience for office gossip. If the general conversation adds nothing to your life, then you'd rather work on your own. Running your own business is an excellent career choice.

You love learning and knowledge too, and you're willing to delve deep to discover more. In fact, your desire to find out about the world and your own personal development and growth knows no limits. Your love of exploration can take you into areas of life that very few people know about. Find your niche and become renowned as an expert.

When it comes to your choice of career, remember that you're all about transformation. Whatever world you're involved in, you won't be happy doing the same thing day in, day out unless you have an end goal, a bigger purpose.

You might be a scientist or a therapist, a criminologist or a make-up artist, but ultimately the quintessential Scorpio character wants to witness change in some shape or form and know that you played an integral part in it.

If you're seeking inspiration for a new job, take a look at the list below, which reveals the traditional careers that come under the Scorpio archetype:

TRADITIONAL SCORPIO CAREERS

sex therapist
bereavement counsellor
tarot card reader
surgeon
psychic
undertaker
private detective
police officer
spy
researcher
plumber

miner
scuba diver
tube driver
stockbroker
tax inspector
clutter clearer
detox specialist
environmentalist
forensic scientist

Your Money and Prosperity

> **KEY CONCEPTS:** the power of money, expert advice, believing what you're worth, money and transcendence

Your relationship with money is an interesting one. You don't necessarily view money as a commodity that can buy you what you want; instead it's what money means to you that's more important.

One concept that most Scorpios understand is a recognition that money equals power. In fact, this holds true for many areas of your life. It's what you can do with money and how it can transform your own and other people's lives that grabs your attention.

You probably realise instinctively that money makes money and you, more than any other sign, may succeed in the world of trading, stocks and shares, property deals, investing in small businesses, etc. You have a sound brain for money matters and finance. You're unlikely to leap into any deal impulsively but instead will think things through carefully and draw up a clear strategy.

You don't usually worry, either, if you don't have all the expertise or knowledge to hand to make your money go further. This is where you know to team up with other people, in joint ventures and business partnerships that can help you grow and make progress quicker than you could on your own. Work with a top accountant or a financial adviser to get the best deals possible.

Other people's money often comes your way at some point in your lifetime, including inheritances, returns on investment, bonuses or gifts of money. You might even be drawn into some dodgy financial deals if you take a wrong turn in life, and could end up having to tackle blackmail or hush money. Keep on the straight and narrow in life.

Money is a private matter for you, and if you're typical of your sign, you won't reveal how much you earn or own readily. This might be because you don't want to give too much away and you know that being secretive about your own affairs has its benefits. It means other people can't take advantage of you easily.

In business, you're likely to push hard for an increase in salary if you believe you deserve it, and you probably know instinctively what you're worth. You have a high regard for money because of the value it represents, and you don't take kindly to being underpaid.

It's also important that at some point in your life you take the next step beyond equating money with power and recognise that ultimately, money is energy. This means trusting that money will come your way when it's needed and, by following the Law of Attraction, being able to increase your money luck.

This can be a difficult concept for you to get hold of at first because ultimately it means letting go of control and putting your trust in the universe. When you do so, however, you start to discover the magic surrounding money and that what you give, you receive in return. This taps into the side of your Scorpio nature that's in tune with meta-physical laws. At your very essence, your core, you're the alchemist who can turn base lead into gold.

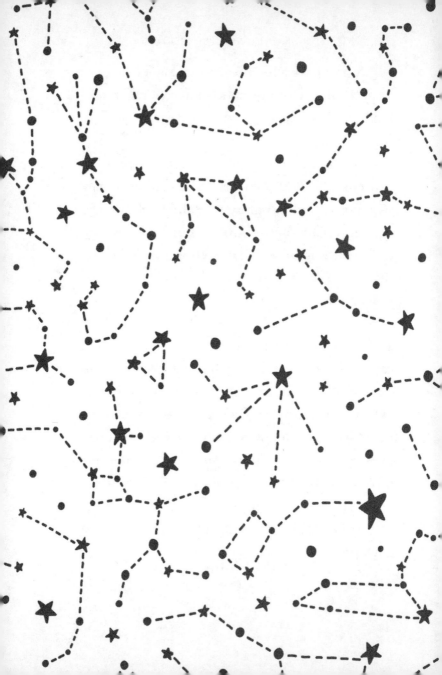

Your Cosmic Gifts and Talents

Keeping A Secret

You are the zodiac archetype of the 'strong, silent type' and you're an expert at keeping things hidden. This doesn't always go down well in your relationships, especially if someone thinks you're being overly secretive or private, but maintaining a secret is your top skill or weapon. In fact, if anyone is to be trusted with a secret, it's you. This can be an enormous asset in many areas of life, so use it to the best of your ability.

Honouring Death

In the western world we're not educated to have a close relationship with death; but if any of the star signs can be said to honour death, it's Scorpio. You know that death isn't the end of the road but rather a transition, moving from one world to the next.

As a Scorpio, you understand that it's when we encounter death in our lives that we feel most deeply. This is also passion. You can help teach people not to steer away from their pain or run from painful emotions but instead, when someone passes away, to celebrate joyfully and mourn fully in equal measure.

Living Intensely

You're a passionate individual who often holds superficial behaviour in disdain. You want the full monty in life, to go in deep and experience all that you can as intensely as possible while you're on this planet. You want to experience the whole gamut of your emotions, you want to stay up all night so you can witness the dawn, you want to push life itself to the limit.

You understand, too, that it's when you dare to open your heart fully and to love completely that you experience life at its fullest and most vibrant intensity.

Being A Survivor

It is relatively rare for a Scorpio to go through life without encountering any transformative personal experiences. In fact, what often pinpoints you as the survivor of the zodiac is the fact that you learn the most and gain strength when you encounter crisis, tragedy or a near-death experience in your own life. In fact, it's quite amazing to find out how many of you Scorpios have lived through challenging times and found the inner strength and resilience to start over. This is an incredible cosmic gift.

Super Sleuth

You're the detective of the zodiac, and if you're a typical Scorpio, you love nothing more than a good mystery to unravel or a puzzle to decode. This is where you can excel in life, whether you're making a scientific breakthrough, you're involved in relevant research, or you're working on a personal project to the point of obsession. If you need someone to get to the core of an issue or to piece together disparate pieces of evidence to solve the crime, it's a Scorpio.

Psychic Ability

Not all Scorpios have psychic ability, but a lot of you do. Paul McKenna (8 November) is one of the top hypnotherapists in the world and has made millions from his self-help books and teaching people about the power of the mind. You might not be a Paul McKenna but what all Scorpios do have is the insight and natural ability to read other people well and even, sometimes, to know what they're thinking.

This can be an excellent skill to have, both personally and professionally. Practise tapping into your sixth sense, trust your natural instincts and go beyond what you believe your mind is capable of.

Healing and Regeneration

You're a natural healer who believes in the power of change and recovery, for self and others. As a Scorpio, you go in deep to find the nugget of gold, to reveal hidden riches. It was probably a Scorpio who discovered that if you pile up an enormous amount of shit, it turns into liquid gold and valuable compost material.

You're an expert at recycling what's old and what's been discarded as you see an object's inherent value. The Japanese art of kintsugi – repairing broken pottery with seams of gold – is soul work, in your eyes. You find the antique heirloom among the pile of junk. You winkle out the sliver of light in the darkest of places, and you understand inherently the meaning of the word transformation.

Films, Books, Music

• • • • •

Films: *The First Wives Club* – 'don't get mad, get everything' – a movie about revenge starring Sun Scorpio Goldie Hawn (21 November), Moon Scorpio Bette Midler and Ascendant Scorpio Diane Keaton; or any film collaborations between Scorpio duo Martin Scorsese (17 November) and Leonardo DiCaprio (11 November), e.g. *The Wolf Of Wall Street*

Books: The James Bond series by Ian Fleming (James Bond is a Scorpio – official birthday, 11 November) or *The Remains of the Day* by Kazuo Ishiguro (8 November)

Music: The Scorpions, the Eagles, Phoenix – all named after Scorpio's zodiac symbols – or any album by 'triple Scorpio', Sun, Moon and Ascendant in Scorpio, Björk (21 November)

YOGA POSE:

Goddess: strengthens the lower body, opens the groin

TAROT CARD:

The Devil

GIFTS TO BUY A SCORPIO:

- a pair of leather gloves
- sexy black lingerie
- the latest detective novel
- a box set of *The Killing*
- a diary with a lock (for your private secrets)
- a night out at an intimate jazz club
- Opium perfume for the women, Hugo Boss for the men

- a copy of the *Kama Sutra*
- chilli pepper – a plant or hot sauce
- Star Gift – a cloak of invisibility

Scorpio Celebrities Born On Your Birthday

OCTOBER

 23 (Ryan Reynolds – born on the cusp, see Q&A)

 24 Kevin Kline, Caprice Bourret, Wayne Rooney, Drake, Bill Wyman, Roman Abramovich

25 Pablo Picasso, David Furnish, Ciara, Katy Perry, Rylan Clark

26 Hillary Clinton, Bob Hoskins, Jaclyn Smith, James Pickens Jr, Rita Wilson, Seth MacFarlane, Dylan McDermott, Keith Urban, Natalie Merchant, Napoleon Hill

27 Dylan Thomas, Sylvia Plath, John Cleese, Kelly Osbourne

28 Evelyn Waugh, Bill Gates, Caitlyn Jenner, Julia Roberts, Cleo Laine, David Dimbleby, Brad Paisley, Joaquin Phoenix

29 Richard Dreyfuss, Winona Ryder, Gabrielle Union, Matt Smith, Rufus Sewell

30 Charles Atlas, Kevin Pollak, Michael Winner, Diego Maradona, Gavin Rossdale, Ivanka Trump, Clémence Poésy

31 John Candy, Peter Jackson, Vanilla Ice, The Cheeky Girls, Dermot Mulroney, Willow Smith

NOVEMBER

1 Lyle Lovett, Jenny McCarthy, Aishwarya Rai, Larry Flynt, Toni Collette

2 Burt Lancaster, k.d. lang, Samantha Janus, Nelly, David Schwimmer, Shahrukh Khan

3 Charles Bronson, Lulu, Anna Wintour, Roseanne Barr, Adam Ant, Kendall Jenner, Dolph Lundgren, Colin Kaepernick

4 P. Diddy, Matthew McConaughey, Louise Redknapp, Kathy Griffin, Robert Mapplethorpe

5 Roy Rogers, Vivien Leigh, Tatum O'Neal, Art Garfunkel, Sam Shepard, Bryan Adams, Tilda Swinton, Sam Rockwell,

Tamzin Outhwaite, Danniella Westbrook, Alexa Chung, Kris Jenner

6 Sally Field, Maria Shriver, Nigel Havers, Ethan Hawke, Thandie Newton, Rebecca Romijn, Nell McAndrew, Emma Stone, Cath Kidston

7 Marie Curie, Billy Graham, Joni Mitchell, Yunjin Kim, Lorde

8 Bram Stoker, Christiaan Barnard, Bonnie Raitt, Paul McKenna, Gordon Ramsay, Tara Reid, Jack Osbourne, Kazuo Ishiguro, Christie Hefner

9 Carl Sagan, Nick Lachey, Vanessa Lachey, Delta Goodrem, Eric Dane, Caroline Flack

10 Richard Burton, Tim Rice, Ellen Pompeo, Hugh Bonneville, Brittany Murphy, Neil Gaiman, Eve

11 James Bond, Kurt Vonnegut, June Whitfield, Kathy Lette, Demi Moore, Calista Flockhart, Leonardo DiCaprio

12 Grace Kelly, Stefanie Powers, Neil Young, Mariella Frostrup, Ryan Gosling, Anne Hathaway, Tonya Harding

13 Whoopi Goldberg, Gerard Butler, Jimmy Kimmel, Lucy Fallon

14 Prince Charles, Condoleezza Rice, Laura San Giacomo, Letitia Dean, Josh Duhamel

15 Paul Raymond, Georgia O'Keeffe, Petula Clark, Dom Joly, Jonny Lee Miller, Shailene Woodley

16 Frank Bruno, Maggie Gyllenhaal, Gemma Atkinson, Griff Rhys Jones, Vicky Pattison

17 Rock Hudson, Martin Scorsese, Lauren Hutton, Danny de Vito, Peter Cook, Jonathan Ross, Sarah Harding, Rachel McAdams, Jeff Buckley, RuPaul, Ore Oduba

18 Margaret Atwood, Linda Evans, Amanda Lear, Kim Wilde, Owen Wilson, Chloe Sevigny, Ant McPartlin, Brené Brown

19 Larry King, Ted Turner, Calvin Klein, Meg Ryan, Jodie Foster, Indira Gandhi, Tyga

20 Alistair Cooke, Bo Derek, Kimberley Walsh

21 Goldie Hawn, Tina Brown, Nicollette Sheridan, Liza Tarbuck, Björk, Carly Rae Jepson

22 Billie Jean King, Jamie Lee Curtis, Boris Becker, Oscar Pistorius, Mark Ruffalo

Q&A Section

• • • • •

Q. What is the difference between a Sun sign and a Star sign?

A. They are the same thing. The Sun spends one month in each of the twelve star signs every year, so if you were born on 1 January, you are a Sun Capricorn. In astronomy, the Sun is termed a star rather than a planet, which is why the two names are interchangeable. The term 'zodiac sign', too, means the same as Sun sign and Star sign and is another way of describing which one of the twelve star signs you are, e.g. Sun Capricorn.

Q. What does it mean if I'm born on the cusp?

A. Being born on the cusp means that you were born on a day when the Sun moves from one of the twelve zodiac signs into the next. However, the Sun doesn't change signs at the same time each year. Sometimes it can be a day earlier or a day later. In the celebrity birthday section of the book, names in brackets mean that this person's birthday falls into this category.

If you know your complete birth data, including the date, time and place you were born, you can find out definitively what Sun sign you are. You do this by either checking an ephemeris (a planetary table) or asking an astrologer. For example, if a baby were born on 20 January 2018, it would be Sun Capricorn if born before 03:09 GMT or Sun Aquarius if born after 03:09 GMT. A year earlier, the Sun left Capricorn a day earlier and entered Aquarius on 19 January 2017, at 21:24 GMT. Each year the time changes are slightly different.

Q. Has my sign of the zodiac changed since I was born?

A. Every now and again, the media talks about a new sign of the zodiac called Ophiuchus and about there now being thirteen signs. This means that you're unlikely to be the same Sun sign as you always thought you were.

This method is based on fixing the Sun's movement to the star constellations in the sky, and is called 'sidereal' astrology. It's used traditionally in India and other Asian countries.

The star constellations are merely namesakes for the twelve zodiac signs. In western astrology, the zodiac is divided into twelve equal parts that are in sync with the seasons. This method is called 'tropical' astrology. The star constellations and the zodiac signs aren't the same.

Astrology is based on a beautiful pattern of symmetry (see Additional Information) and it wouldn't be the same if a thirteenth sign were introduced into the pattern. So never fear, no one is going to have to say their star sign is Ophiuchus, a name nobody even knows how to pronounce!

Q. Is astrology still relevant to me if I was born in the southern hemisphere?

A. Yes, astrology is unquestionably relevant to you. Astrology's origins, however, were founded in the northern hemisphere, which is why the Spring Equinox coincides with the Sun's move into Aries, the first sign of the zodiac. In the southern hemisphere, the seasons are reversed. Babylonian, Egyptian and Greek and Roman astrology are the forebears of modern-day astrology, and all of these civilisations were located in the northern hemisphere.

• • • • •

Q. Should I read my Sun sign, Moon sign and Ascendant sign?

A. If you know your horoscope or you have drawn up an astrology wheel for the time of your birth, you will be aware that you are more than your Sun sign. The Sun is the most important star in the sky, however, because the other planets revolve around it, and your horoscope in the media is based on Sun signs. The Sun represents your essence, who you are striving to become throughout your lifetime.

The Sun, Moon and Ascendant together give you a broader impression of yourself as all three reveal further elements about your personality. If you know your Moon and Ascendant signs, you can read all three books to gain further insight into who you are. It's also a good idea to read the Sun sign book that relates to your partner, parents, children, best friends, even your boss for a better understanding of their characters too.

Q. Is astrology a mix of fate and free will?

A. Yes. Astrology is not causal, i.e. the planets don't cause things to happen in your life; instead, the two are interconnected, hence the saying 'As above, so below'. The symbolism of the planets' movements mirrors what's happening on earth and in your personal experience of life.

You can choose to sit back and let your life unfold, or you can decide the best course of action available to you. In this way, you are combining your fate and free will, and this is one of astrology's major purposes in life. A knowledge of astrology can help you live more authentically, and it offers you a fresh perspective on how best to make progress in your life.

Q. What does it mean if I don't identify with my Sun sign? Is there a reason for this?

A. The majority of people identify with their Sun sign, and it is thought that one route to fulfilment is to grow into your Sun sign. You do get the odd exception, however.

For example, a Pisces man was adamant that he wasn't at all romantic, mystical, creative or caring, all typical Pisces archetypes. It turned out he'd spent the whole of his adult life working in the oil industry and lived primarily on the sea. Neptune is one of Pisces' ruling planets and god of the sea and Pisces rules all liquids, including oil. There's the Pisces connection.

Q. What's the difference between astrology and astronomy?

A. Astrology means 'language of the stars', whereas astronomy means 'mapping of the stars'. Traditionally, they were considered one discipline, one form of study and they coexisted together for many hundreds of years. Since the dawn of the Scientific Age, however, they have split apart.

Astronomy is the scientific strand, calculating and logging the movement of the planets, whereas astrology is the interpretation of the movement of the stars. Astrology works on a symbolic and intuitive level to offer guidance and insight. It reunites you with a universal truth, a knowingness that can sometimes get lost in place of an objective, scientific truth. Both are of value.

Q. What is a cosmic marriage in astrology?

A. One of the classic indicators of a relation-ship that's a match made in heaven is the union of the Sun and Moon. When they fall close to each other in the same sign in the birth charts of you and your partner, this is called a cosmic marriage. In astrology, the Sun and Moon are the king and queen of the heavens; the Sun is a masculine energy, and the Moon a feminine energy. They represent the eternal cycle of day and night, yin and yang.

Q. What does the Saturn Return mean?

A. In traditional astrology, Saturn was the furthest planet from the Sun, representing boundaries and the end of the universe. Saturn is linked to karma and time, and represents authority, structure and responsibility. It takes Saturn twenty-nine to thirty years to make a complete cycle of the zodiac and return to the place where it was when you were born.

This is what people mean when they talk about their Saturn Return; it's the astrological coming of age. Turning thirty can be a soul-searching time, when you examine how far you've come in life and whether you're on the right track. It's a watershed moment, a reality check and a defining stage of adulthood. The decisions you make during your Saturn Return are crucial, whether they represent endings or new commitments. Either way, it's the start of an important stage in your life path.

Additional Information

· · · · ·

The Symmetry of Astrology

There is a beautiful symmetry to the zodiac (see horoscope wheel). There are twelve zodiac signs, which can be divided into two sets of 'introvert' and 'extrovert' signs, four elements (fire, earth, air, water), three modes (cardinal, fixed, mutable) and six pairs of opposite signs.

One of the values of astrology is in bringing opposites together, showing how they complement each other and work together and, in so doing, restore unity. The horoscope wheel represents the cyclical nature of life.

Aries (*March 21–April 19*)
Taurus (*April 20–May 20*)
Gemini (*May 21–June 20*)
Cancer (*June 21–July 22*)
Leo (*July 23–August 22*)
Virgo (*August 23–September 22*)
Libra (*September 23–October 23*)
Scorpio (*October 24–November 22*)
Sagittarius (*November 23–December 21*)
Capricorn (*December 22–January 20*)
Aquarius (*January 21–February 18*)
Pisces (*February 19–March 20*)

ELEMENTS

There are four elements in astrology and three signs allocated to each. The elements are:

fire – Aries, Leo, Sagittarius
earth – Taurus, Virgo, Capricorn
air – Gemini, Libra, Aquarius
water – Cancer, Scorpio, Pisces

What each element represents:

Fire – fire blazes bright and fire types are inspirational, motivational, adventurous and love creativity and play

Earth – earth is grounding and solid, and earth rules money, security, practicality, the physical body and slow living

Air – air is intangible and vast and air rules thinking, ideas, social interaction, debate and questioning

Water – water is deep and healing and water rules feelings, intuition, quietness, relating, giving and sharing

MODES

There are three modes in astrology and four star signs allocated to each. The modes are:

cardinal – Aries, Cancer, Libra, Capricorn
fixed – Taurus, Leo, Scorpio, Aquarius
mutable – Gemini, Virgo, Sagittarius, Pisces

What each mode represents:

Cardinal – The first group represents the leaders of the zodiac, and these signs love to initiate and take action. Some say they're controlling.

Fixed – The middle group holds fast and stands the middle ground and acts as a stable, reliable companion. Some say they're stubborn.

Mutable – The last group is more willing to go with the flow and let life drift. They're more flexible and adaptable and often dual-natured. Some say they're all over the place.

INTROVERT AND EXTROVERT SIGNS/ OPPOSITE SIGNS

The introvert signs are the earth and water signs and the extrovert signs are the fire and air signs. Both sets oppose each other across the zodiac.

The 'introvert' earth and water oppositions are:

- Taurus – • Scorpio
- Cancer – • Capricorn
- Virgo – • Pisces

The 'extrovert' air and fire oppositions are:

- Aries – · Libra
- Gemini – · Sagittarius
- Leo – · Aquarius

THE HOUSES

The houses of the astrology wheel are an additional component to Sun sign horoscopes. The symmetry that is inherent within astrology remains, as the wheel is divided into twelve equal sections, called 'houses'. Each of the twelve houses is governed by one of the twelve zodiac signs.

There is an overlap in meaning as you move round the houses. Once you know the symbolism of all the star signs, it can be fleshed out further by learning about the areas of life represented by the twelve houses.

The houses provide more specific information if you choose to have a detailed birth chart reading.

This is based not only on your day of birth, which reveals your star sign, but also your time and place of birth. Here's the complete list of the meanings of the twelve houses and the zodiac sign they are ruled by:

1 – **Aries:** self, physical body, personal goals

2 – **Taurus:** money, possessions, values

3 – **Gemini:** communication, education, siblings, local neighbourhood

4 – **Cancer:** home, family, roots, the past, ancestry

5 – **Leo:** creativity, romance, entertainment, children, luck

6 – **Virgo:** work, routine, health, service

7 – **Libra:** relationships, the 'other', enemies, contracts

8 – **Scorpio:** joint finances, other peoples' resources, all things hidden and taboo

9 – **Sagittarius:** travel, study, philosophy, legal affairs, publishing, religion

10 – **Capricorn:** career, vocation, status, reputation

11 – **Aquarius:** friends, groups, networks, social responsibilities

12 – **Pisces:** retreat, sacrifice, spirituality

A GUIDE TO LOVE MATCHES

The star signs relate to each other in different ways depending on their essential nature. It can also be helpful to know the pattern they create across the zodiac. Here's a quick guide that relates to the chapter on Love Matches:

Two Peas In A Pod – the same star sign

Opposites Attract – star signs opposite each other

Soulmates – five or seven signs apart, and a traditional 'soulmate' connection

In Your Element – four signs apart, which means you share the same element

Squaring Up To Each Other – three signs apart, which means you share the same mode

Sexy Sextiles – two signs apart, which means you're both 'introverts' or 'extroverts'

Next Door Neighbours – one sign apart, different in nature but often share close connections